Rookie
Read-About®
Science

How Do You Know
It's Fall?

by Lisa M. Herrington

Content Consultant
Randy C. Bilik, M.A.
Julia A. Stark Elementary School, Stamford, Connecticut

Reading Consultant
Jeanne M. Clidas, Ph.D.
Reading Specialist

Children's Press®
An Imprint of Scholastic Inc.
New York Toronto London Auckland Sydney
Mexico City New Delhi Hong Kong
Danbury, Connecticut

Library of Congress Cataloging-in-Publication Data
Herrington, Lisa M., author.
  How do you know it's fall? / by Lisa M. Herrington.
    pages cm. — (Rookie read-about science)
  Summary: "Introduces the reader to the fall season."—Provided by publisher.
  Audience: 3-6.
  Includes index.
  ISBN 978-0-531-29946-3 (library binding) — ISBN 978-0-531-22575-2 (pbk.)
  1. Autumn—Juvenile literature. I. Title. II. Title: How do you know it is fall?
  III. Series: Rookie read-about science.
  QB637.7.H474 2014
  508.2—dc23   2013014926

Produced by Spooky Cheetah Press

© 2014 by Scholastic Inc.

All rights reserved. Published in 2014 by Children's Press, an imprint of Scholastic Inc.

Printed in China 62

SCHOLASTIC, CHILDREN'S PRESS, ROOKIE READ-ABOUT®, and associated logos
are trademarks and/or registered trademarks of Scholastic Inc.

23 22 21 20 19 18 17 R 26 25 24 23

Photos ©: cover: Jose Luis Pelaez/Media Bakery; 3 top left: dibrova/Getty Images;
3 top right: caelmi/Getty Images; 4: Graham Oliver/Media Bakery; 7: Bill Brooks/
Alamy Images; 11: Andrew Olney/Media Bakery; 12: Sparkmom/Dreamstime; 16:
Ginosphotos/Dreamstime; 19: Media Bakery; 20: Fancy/Media Bakery; 23: Media
Bakery; 24: Ariel Skelley/Media Bakery; 28: rossario/Getty Images; 29: Graham
Oliver/Media Bakery; 30: Adam Chinitz; 31 top: Ginosphotos/Dreamstime; 31 center
top: Ariel Skelley/Media Bakery; 31 center bottom: Media Bakery; 31 bottom: Fancy/
Media Bakery.

All other photos © Shutterstock.

Table of Contents

Welcome, Fall!

Leaves change colors.
Birds fly south.
Pumpkins are ready to be picked.
That is how we know it is fall!

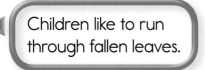

Children like to run through fallen leaves.

There are four seasons in each year. Each season lasts about three months. Fall is the season that comes after summer. Another name for fall is autumn.

FUN FACT!

The first day of fall is September 22nd or 23rd.

Winter

Spring

Summer

Fall

What's the Weather?

In some areas, the air gets cooler in fall. There is less sunlight at this time of year. The days become shorter as the sun goes down earlier each night.

FUN FACT!

On the first day of fall, day and night are each about 12 hours long.

Fall can be windy and chilly.
We wear pants, sweaters, and
coats to stay warm.

This boy and his father
are dressed for a fall walk.

Plants and Animals in Fall

Fall bursts with color. Some leaves turn red, orange, yellow, and brown. Then they drop off the trees.

FUN FACT!

Leaves change colors because there is less sunlight in fall.

Animals use this time to get ready for winter. Many store food for the cold weather ahead. Squirrels hide nuts and acorns.

This squirrel has gathered nuts for winter.

Some birds **migrate**. They leave for warmer winter homes. You might hear a **flock** of geese honking in the sky.

A flock of geese flies in the shape of the letter V.

Monarch butterflies also migrate. They journey to warmer places during the cold winter months.

FUN FACT!

Monarchs fly to California and Mexico for the winter.

Kids in Fall

Many crops are ready to be eaten in fall. We can pick **ripe** apples from trees. Yum! Apples are crunchy and sweet.

To find out if apples sink or float, try the experiment on page 30.

In October, we pick pumpkins from a patch. We carve them into jack-o'-lanterns. On Halloween, we dress up in costumes. We go trick-or-treating.

FUN FACT!

Pumpkins start out as seeds and grow on vines.

In late November, we **celebrate** another fall holiday—Thanksgiving. We eat a big turkey meal with our family. We give thanks for all the good things in our lives.

FUN FACT!

Thanksgiving takes place on the fourth Thursday in November.

Kids are back in school in fall. This is also time for playing football, taking hikes, and riding bikes.

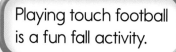

Playing touch football is a fun fall activity.

Let's Explore!

- Look at the picture. What do you see that tells you fall has arrived?

- Take a nature walk outside in fall. What clues can you find in your yard or neighborhood that say fall is here?

- In a science journal, draw pictures of what you observed. Write down some words that describe what you saw, heard, and smelled.

We rake leaves into piles. We have fun jumping in the piles. What is *your* favorite thing to do in fall?

Sink or Float?

What You'll Need

- A large bowl
- An apple
- A rock

Directions

 1. Fill the bowl with water.

2. Place the apple and the rock, one at a time, in the bowl. Before you place each object, guess whether it will sink or float.

3. Observe what happens.

Think About It: Did the apple float? Why do you think that is? Did the rock float? Why or why not?

Answer: Apples float because they are made up of a lot of air, which makes them lighter than the water. A rock is solid all the way through. Even small pebbles are heavier than water.

Glossary

celebrate (SEH-luh-brayt): to do something fun on a special occasion

flock (FLOK): a group of animals that live, travel, or feed together

migrate (MY-grayt): to move from one place to another in search of warmth or food

ripe (RIPE): ready to be picked or eaten

Index

About the Author

Lisa M. Herrington is a freelance writer and editor. Lisa lives in Trumbull, Connecticut, with her husband, Ryan, and her daughter, Caroline. She loves everything about fall—crisp weather, colorful leaves, and pumpkin patches!